Collins

Easy Le

Phonics
Workbook 1

Age 5-7

This book belongs to

_____ .

How to use this book

- Easy Learning workbooks help your child improve basic skills, build confidence and develop a love of learning.

- Find a quiet, comfortable place to work, away from distractions.

- Get into a routine of completing one or two workbook pages with your child every day.

- Ask your child to circle the star that matches how many activities they have completed on every page:

Some = half of the activities

Most = more than half

All = all the activities

- The progress certificate at the back of this book will help you and your child keep track of how many have been circled.

- Encourage your child to work through all of the activities eventually, and praise them for completing the progress certificate.

- Each workbook builds on the previous one in the series. Help your child complete this one to ensure they have covered what they need to know before starting the next workbook.

Parent tips

- It's vital that your child learns the correct sound for each of the letters in this book. Work through the book with your child. Reinforce the correct letter sounds as they progress and help them with any words they may be unable to read.

Parent tip
Look out for tips to help your child learn the correct sounds for the letters.

- Ask your child to find and colour the little monkeys that are hidden throughout this book.

- This will help engage them with the pages of the book and get them interested in the activities.

(Don't count this one.)

Published by Collins
An imprint of HarperCollins*Publishers*
77–85 Fulham Palace Road
Hammersmith
London
W6 8JB

Browse the complete Collins catalogue at
www.collinseducation.com

First published in 2012
© HarperCollins*Publishers* 2012

10 9 8 7 6 5 4 3 2 1

ISBN-13 978-0-00-746731-0

British Library Cataloguing in Publication Data

A catalogue record for this publication is available from the British Library

Design and layout by Linda Miles, Lodestone Publishing
Illustrated by Steve Evans, Jenny Tulip, Rachel Annie Bridgen, Graham Smith, Andy Tudor and Kathy Baxendale
Cover design by Linda Miles
Cover illustration by Kathy Baxendale
Commissioned by Tammy Poggo
Project managed by Katie Galloway
Printed in China

MIX
Paper from responsible sources
FSC
www.fsc.org
FSC C007454

FSC™ is a non-profit international organisation established to promote the responsible management of the world's forests. Products carrying the FSC label are independently certified to assure consumers that they come from forests that are managed to meet the social, economic and ecological needs of present and future generations, and other controlled sources.

Find out more about HarperCollins and the environment at
www.harpercollins.co.uk/green

Contents

Letters s, a, t and p

1 Say the letters. Write the letters.

s   a   t   p

2 Write **s**, **a**, **t** or **p** to finish the words.

 _____ap

 _____ock

 _____pple

 _____un

 _____nt

 _____encil

3 Write the letter that each picture begins with.

 ☐    ☐   ☐   ☐

4 Do each word sum to make a word.

s + a + t = _____

t + a + p = _____

How much did you do?   Activities 1–4

Circle the star to show what you have done.

 Some   Most   All

Letters i, n, m and d

1 Say the letters. Write the letters.

2 Write **i, n, m** or **d** to finish the words.

_____gloo

_____onkey

_____ish

_____nk

_____et

_____ose

3 Write the letter each picture begins with.

☐   ☐   ☐   ☐

4 Do each word sum to make a word.

m + a + t = _____

m + a + n = _____

Parent tip
Make sure your child knows the correct sounds for the letters on this page, for example: **i**nk, **n**et, **m**op, **d**og.

How much did you do?   Activities 1–4

Circle the star to show what you have done.

 Some

 Most

 All

Letters g, o, c and k

1 Say the letters. Write the letters.

g   o   c   k

2 Write **g, o, c** or **k** to finish the words.

_____range

_____ate

_____ey

_____ow

_____tter

_____ing

3 Write the letter each picture begins with.

▢   ▢   ▢   ▢

4 Do each word sum to make a word.

g + o = _____

k + i + d = _____

How much did you do?   Activities 1–4

Circle the star to show what you have done.

 Some

 Most

 All

Letters e, u and r

1 Say the letters. Write the letters.

2 Write **e, u** or **r** to finish the words.

 _____p

 _____abbit

 _____gg

 _____ing

 _____nder

 _____nvelope

3 Write the letter each picture begins with.

  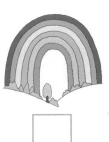

☐   ☐   ☐

4 Do each word sum to make a word.

n + e + t = _____

u + p = _____

How much did you do?

Activities 1–4

Circle the star to show what you have done.

 Some

 Most

 All

Letters h, b and f

1 Say the letters. Write the letters.

h   b   f

2 Write **h**, **b** or **f** to finish the words.

_____inger

_____at

_____at

_____orse

_____eather

_____ed

3 Write the letter each picture begins with.

□   □   □

4 Do each word sum to make a word.

f + i + t = _____

h + o + t = _____

Parent tip
Make sure your child knows the correct sounds for the letters on this page, for example: **h**at, **b**ed, **f**ish.

How much did you do?   ## Activities 1–4

Circle the star to show what you have done.

Some

Most

All

Letters l, j and v

1 Say the letters. Write the letters.

2 Write **l**, **j** or **v** to finish the words.

_____ug

_____etter

_____amp

_____an

_____iolin

_____elly

3 Write the letter each picture begins with.

4 Do each word sum to make a word.

j + u + g = _____

v + a + n = _____

How much did you do?   Activities 1–4

Circle the star to show what you have done.

 Some

 Most

 All

Letters w, x, y and z

1 Say the letters. Write the letters.

w   x   y   z

2 Write **w, x, y** or **z** to finish the words.

 _____ell

6 si_____

 _____olk

 _____eb

 _____ebra

 _____indow

3 Write the letter each picture begins with.

 ☐

 ☐

 ☐

 ☐

4 Do each word sum to make a word.

y + e + s = _____

w + e + t = _____

> **Parent tip**
> Make sure your child knows the correct sounds for the letters on this page, for example: **w**eb, **x**-ray, **y**ellow, **z**ip.

How much did you do?   Activities 1–4

Circle the star to show what you have done.

 Some

 Most

 All

Letters ff, ll, ss and zz

1 Say the letters. Write the letters.

2 Write **ff, ll, ss** or **zz** to finish the words.

me_____   se_____   ja_____   pu_____

3 Write the double letters each picture ends with.

☐   ☐   ☐   ☐

4 Do each word sum to make a word.

d + o + ll = _____

h + u + ff = _____

b + u + zz = _____

l + e + ss = _____

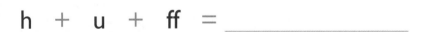

Parent tip
Make sure your child knows the correct sounds for the letters on this page, for example: puff, bell, boss, buzz.

How much did you do?   Activities 1–4

Circle the star
to show what
you have done.

Some   Most   All

ck and qu words

1 Say the words. Write the letters.

so**ck**

quiz

---

2 Write the **ck** or **qu** letters that each picture begins or ends with.

---

3 Do each word sum to make a word.

d + u + ck = _____

qu + i + ck = _____

s + o + ck = _____

qu + i + z = _____

---

4 Draw lines to the right answers.

It tells the time.   queen

An important lady.   clock

How much did you do?   ## Activities 1–4

Circle the star to show what you have done.

 Some

 Most

 All

ch words

1 Say the word. Write the letters.

chip

2 Do each word sum to make a word.

ch + i + p = _____

ch + i + n = _____

ch + i + ck = _____

ch + a + t = _____

ch + o + p = _____

> **Parent tip**
> Make sure your child knows the correct sound for the letters on this page, for example: **ch**urn.

3 Look at the words you have written in **2**.
Write the correct word next to each clue.

A part of your face   _____

A cooked piece of potato   _____

A piece of meat   _____

A baby hen   _____

To talk   _____

How much did you do?   Activities 1–3

Circle the star
to show what
you have done.

 Some

 Most

 All

sh words

1 Say the word. Write the letters.

sheep

2 Do each word sum to make a word.

sh + i + p = _____

sh + o + p = _____

d + i + sh = _____

f + i + sh = _____

sh + i + n = _____

Parent tip
Make sure your child knows the correct sound for the letters on this page, for example: **sh**eep.

3 Look at the words you have written in **2** .
Write the correct word next to each clue.

It sells things. _____

It floats on water. _____

It swims in water. _____

It is part of your leg. _____

It can have food in it. _____

How much did you do?   Activities 1–3

Circle the star
to show what
you have done.

Some

Most

All

th words

1 Say the word. Write the letters.

ba**th**

2 Do each word sum to make a word.

th + i + n = _____

th + i + ck = _____

p + a + th = _____

b + a + th = _____

th + u + d = _____

> **Parent tip**
> Make sure your child knows the correct sound for the letters on this page, for example: **th**in.

3 Look at the words you have written in **2**.
Write the correct word next to each clue.

The opposite of thin. _____

You walk along it. _____

A dull sound. _____

The opposite of thick. _____

You put water in it. _____

How much did you do? Activities 1–3

Circle the star to show what you have done.

 Some

 Most

 All

15

ai words

1 Say the word. Write the letters.

tail _ai_

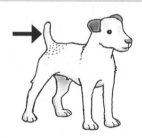

2 Use a word from the box to finish each sentence.

Darren wanted to **s**_____ to the island.

The **r**_____ soaked Tina.

My dog had an itch in his **t**_____.

As the **h**_____ fell it made a lot of noise.

| rain |
| hail |
| sail |
| tail |

Parent tip
Make sure your child knows the correct sound for the letters on this page, for example: tail.

3 Sort the **ai** words into the table.

maid   snail   train   paid   rain   laid   tail   drain   sail

ain words	**ail** words	**aid** words

4 Write your own sentence with an **ai** word.

_____

How much did you do?   Activities 1–4

Circle the star to show what you have done.

Some

Most

All

ee words

1 Say the word. Write the letters.

fe**e**t _ee_ . .

2 Use a word from the box to finish each sentence.

The **s**_____ is planted into the soil.

Dig that **w**_____ up!

My **f**_____ were sore after the long walk.

Dan began to **w**_____ quietly after he fell over.

| weed |
| feet |
| seed |
| weep |

3 Sort the **ee** words into the table.

feet   bleed   jeep   feed   meet   sheep   sweet   need   creep

eed words	**eet** words	**eep** words

4 Write your own sentence with an **ee** word.

_____

How much did you do?   Activities 1–4

Circle the star to show what you have done.

Some   Most   All

igh words

1 Say the word. Write the letters.

light

2 Use a word from the box to finish each sentence.

Paul's glasses help his **s**_____.

My cat is stuck **h**_____ up in the tree.

My dad always snores at **n**_____.

Meena got all her spellings **r**_____.

night
sight
high
right

Parent tip
Make sure your child knows the correct sound for the letters on this page, for example: **ligh**t.

3 Sort the **igh** words into the table.

high   fight   tight   sigh   thigh   might

igh words	**ight** words

4 Write three more **igh** words.

How much did you do?   **Activities 1–4**

Circle the star to show what you have done.

Some

Most

All

18

oa words

1 Say the word. Write the letters.

goat

2 Use a word from the box to finish each sentence.

Mum said I had to use **s**＿＿＿＿＿＿＿ on my face.

We ate a **l**＿＿＿＿＿＿＿ of bread for lunch.

My Gran always **m**＿＿＿＿＿＿＿ if it is cold.

The children love to row the **b**＿＿＿＿＿＿＿ .

| soap |
| boat |
| moans |
| loaf |

Parent tip
Make sure your child knows the correct sound for the letters on this page, for example: b**oa**t.

3 Sort the **oa** words into the table.

boat   coast   coat   load   roast   goat   toad   road   toast

oad words	**oast** words	**oat** words

4 Write your own sentence with an **oa** word.

＿＿＿＿＿＿＿＿＿＿＿＿＿＿＿＿＿＿＿＿＿＿＿＿＿＿＿＿＿＿＿

How much did you do?   Activities 1–4

Circle the star to show what you have done.

 Some   Most   All

19

oo words

1 Say the word. Write the letters.

moon ⟨⟨oo⟩⟩ . .

2 Use a word from the box to finish each sentence.

The pony had a sore **h**_____.

The **m**_____ shone through my window at night.

The party **f**_____ looked tasty.

My dog dug up the flower's **r**_____!

food
moon
roots
hoof

3 Sort the **oo** words into the table.

boot   moon   shoot   room   soon   root   broom   spoon   zoom

oon words	**oom** words	**oot** words

4 Write three more **oo** words.
Make sure the **oo** sound is the same as the **oo** in m**oo**n.

How much did you do?

Activities 1–4

Circle the star to show what you have done.

Some   Most   All

ar and er words

1 Say the words. Write the letters.

car   ar   ladder   er

2 Add **ar** or **er** to make a word.

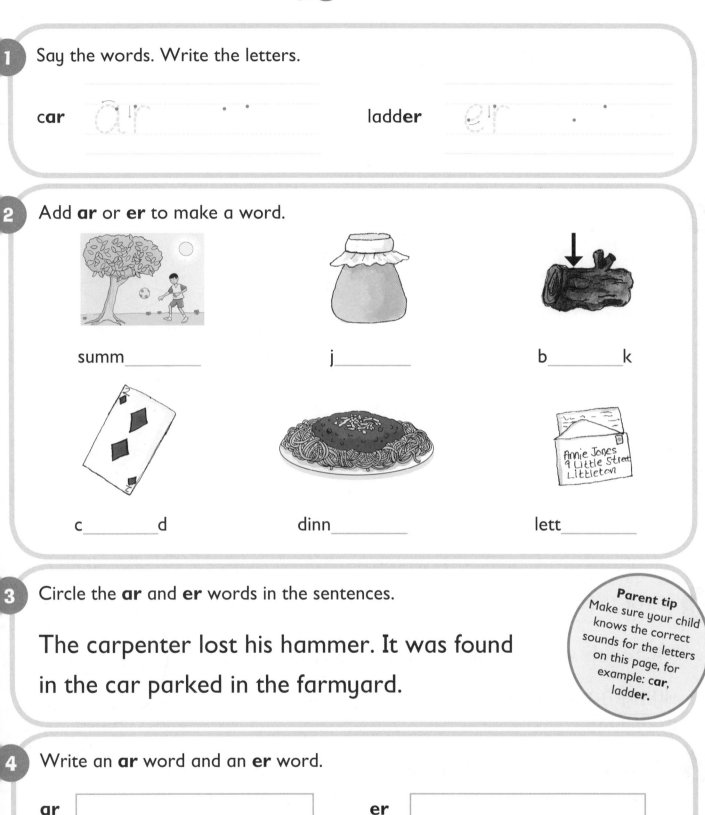

summ_____   j_____   b_____k

c_____d   dinn_____   lett_____

3 Circle the **ar** and **er** words in the sentences.

The carpenter lost his hammer. It was found in the car parked in the farmyard.

> **Parent tip**
> Make sure your child knows the correct sounds for the letters on this page, for example: c**ar**, ladd**er**.

4 Write an **ar** word and an **er** word.

ar [   ]   er [   ]

How much did you do?   Activities 1–4

Circle the star to show what you have done.

 Some

 Most

 All

or and ur words

1 Say the words. Write the letters.

cork or   surf ur

2 Add **or** or **ur** to make a word.

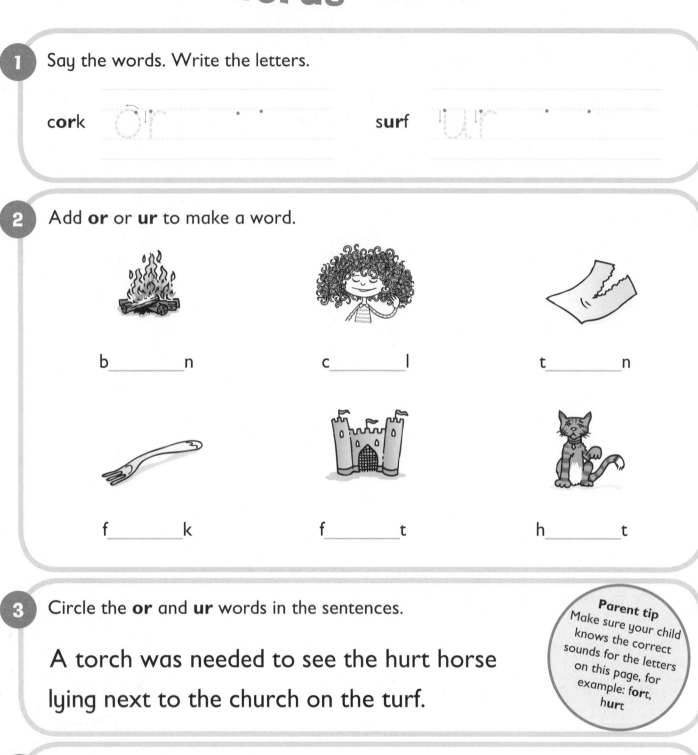

b_____n   c_____l   t_____n

f_____k   f_____t   h_____t

3 Circle the **or** and **ur** words in the sentences.

A torch was needed to see the hurt horse
lying next to the church on the turf.

> **Parent tip**
> Make sure your child knows the correct sounds for the letters on this page, for example: **fort**, **hurt**

4 Write an **or** word and an **ur** word.

or [   ]   ur [   ]

How much did you do?   Activities 1–4

Circle the star
to show what
you have done.

Some

Most

All

ow words

1 Say the word. Write the letters.

owl O W

2 Draw lines to join the words that rhyme.

down   prowl

how   town

owl   cow

3 Finish each sentence with an **ow** word.

The **cl**_____**n** is funny.

The _____**l** flew towards the moon.

Pearson has a **br**_____**n** coat.

4 Write two **ow** words.
Make sure the **ow** sound is the same as the **ow** in **cow**.

How much did you do?   Activities 1–4

Circle the star to show what you have done.

☆ Some   ★ Most   ★ All

oi words

1 Say the word. Write the letters.

b**oi**l   oi . .

2 Draw lines to join the words that rhyme.

boil   point

join   soil

joint   choice

voice   coin

3 Circle the **oi** words in the sentences.

Hannah's garden was spoilt when the soil was flooded. She had no choice. She had to wait until it had dried.

4 Write two **oi** words.

How much did you do?   Activities 1–4

Circle the star to show what you have done.

 Some

 Most

All

ear words

1 Say the word. Write the letters.

ear   _ear_ . . . .

Parent tip
Make sure your child knows the correct sound for the letters on this page, for example: f**ear**.

2 Use the words in the box to label the picture.

ear   beard   tear

3 Finish each sentence with an **ear** word from the box.

fear   hear   near

Ali's school was _____ to his house.

Anna could _____ her mum calling.

Terry felt _____ as he woke in the dark room.

4 Write two **ear** words.
Make sure the **ear** sound is the same as the **ear** in b**ear**d.

How much did you do?   Activities 1–4

Circle the star to show what you have done.

 Some

 Most

 All

air words

1 Say the word. Write the letters.

h**air**   air   · · ·

Parent tip
Make sure your child knows the correct sound for the letters on this page, for example: st**air**.

2 Draw a line to link each word with its matching picture.

pair

chair

stair

3 Circle the **air** words in the sentence.

A brush with fair hair has fallen down the stairs and landed on a chair.

4 Write these two **air** words in your own sentences.

pair   _____

chair   _____

How much did you do?   Activities 1–4

Circle the star to show what you have done.

 Some

 Most

All

nk, nd and ng words

Say the words. Write the letters.

pink nk   pond nd   song ng

Add **nk, nd** or **ng** to make a word.

si_____   sa_____   ri_____

> **Parent tip**
> Make sure your child knows the correct sounds for the letters on this page, for example: i**nk**, ha**nd**, ri**ng**.

i_____   ki_____   ha_____

Write two **nk, nd** and **ng** words.

nk words	**nd** words	**ng** words

How much did you do?   ## Activities 1–3

Circle the star
to show what
you have done.

 Some   Most   All

l blends

1 Say the words. Write the letters.

flag    **cl**ap   **sl**ip

2 Write the words into the table.

flat   slam   blot   flip   plum   blob   slug   plus

bl words	**fl** words
pl words	**sl** words

3 Finish each sentence using a word from the table in ②.

Jason found a _____ in the garden.

Amber ate a _____ as a snack.

Parent tip
Make sure your chil[d]
knows the correct
sounds for the letters
on this page, for
example: **cl**ap.

4 Write words beginning with each of the l blends.

cl _____   **pl** _____   **sl** _____

How much did you do?   Activities 1–4

Circle the star
to show what
you have done.

Some

Most

All

r blends

1 Say the words. Write the letters.

crab ____ drum ____ frog ____

2 Write the words into the table.

pram   trip   gran   drop   trot   prod   grip   drag

dr words	**gr** words
pr words	**tr** words

3 Finish each sentence with a word from the table in ②.

Kate pushed the baby in the _____.

Mr Mead's class went on a _____ to London.

Parent tip
Make sure your child knows the correct sounds for the letters on this page, for example: **trip**.

4 Write words beginning with each of the **r** blends.

dr _____   cr _____   tr _____

How much did you do?   Activities 1–4

Circle the star
to show what
you have done.

Some   Most   All

29

s blends

1 Say the words. Write the letters.

spot sp · ·   **st**ep st · ·   **sw**im sw · ·

2 Write the words into the table.

spin   stop   snail   swim   snap   spot   swing   step

sn words	sp words
st words	sw words

3 Finish each sentence with a word from the table in **2**.

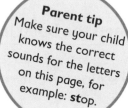

Chloe played on the _____.

"_____!" shouted the policeman.

Parent tip
Make sure your child knows the correct sounds for the letters on this page, for example: **st**op.

4 Write words beginning with each of the **s** blends.

sn _____   st _____   sw _____

How much did you do?   Activities 1–4

Circle the star
to show what
you have done.

Some

Most

All

Words to learn

1 Finish each sentence with a word from the box. You can use the words more than once.

> you   all   be   are
>
> we   for   have   one
>
> said   so   they

H_____ w_____ eaten **a**_____ the sweets?

Joe looked **f**_____ a ball.

Y_____ s_____ he could **h**_____ a drink.

Shall **w**_____ wait **f**_____ them?

T_____ **a**_____ went **f**_____ a walk.

2 Write each of these words in a sentence.

said   _____

be   _____

all   _____

they   _____

How much did you do?   Activities 1–2

Circle the star
to show what
you have done.

 Some   Most   All

Answers

Letters s, a, t and p
Page 4
1 Child's correct pronunciation and writing.
2 tap sock apple sun ant pencil
3 a t p s
4 sat tap

Letters i, n, m and d
Page 5
1 Child's correct pronunciation and writing.
2 igloo monkey dish ink net nose
3 n m i d
4 mat man

Letters g, o, c and k
Page 6
1 Child's correct pronunciation and writing.
2 orange gate key cow otter king
3 o c g k
4 go kid

Letters e, u and r
Page 7
1 Child's correct pronunciation and writing.
2 up rabbit egg ring under envelope
3 e u r
4 net up

Letters h, b and f
Page 8
1 Child's correct pronunciation and writing.
2 finger hat bat horse feather bed
3 f b h
4 fit hot

Letters l, j and v
Page 9
1 Child's correct pronunciation and writing.
2 jug letter lamp van violin jelly
3 l j v
4 jug van

Letters w, x, y and z
Page 10
1 Child's correct pronunciation and writing.
2 yell six yolk web zebra window
3 x w z y
4 yes wet

Letters ff, ll, ss and zz
Page 11
1 Child's correct pronunciation and writing.
2 mess sell jazz puff
3 zz ff ll ss
4 doll huff buzz less

ck and qu words
Page 12
1 Child's correct pronunciation and writing.
2 qu qu ck ck
3 duck quick sock quiz
4 It tells the time – clock
An important lady – queen

ch words
Page 13
1 Child's correct pronunciation and writing.
2 chip chin chick chat chop
3 chin chip chop chick chat

sh words
Page 14
1 Child's correct pronunciation and writing.
2 ship shop dish fish shin
3 shop ship fish shin dish

th words
Page 15
1 Child's correct pronunciation and writing.
2 thin thick path bath thud
3 thick path thud thin bath

ai words
Page 16
1 Child's correct pronunciation and writing.
2 Darren wanted to **sail** to the island.
The **rain** soaked Tina.

My dog had an itch in his **tail**.
As the **hail** fell it made a lot of noise.

3
ain words	ail words	aid words
train	snail	maid
rain	tail	paid
drain	sail	laid

4 Child's own sentence using an **ai** word.

ee words
Page 17
1 Child's correct pronunciation and writing.
2 The **seed** is planted into the soil.
Dig that **weed** up!
My **feet** were sore after the long walk.
Dan began to **weep** quietly after he fell over.

3
eed words	eet words	eep words
bleed	feet	jeep
feed	meet	sheep
need	sweet	creep

4 Child's own sentence using an **ee** word.

igh words
Page 18
1 Child's correct pronunciation and writing.
2 Paul's glasses help his **sight**.
My cat is stuck **high** up in the tree.
My dad always snores at **night**.
Meena got all her spellings **right**.

3
igh words	ight words
high	fight
sigh	tight
thigh	might

4 Three of the child's own **igh** words.

oa words
Page 19
1 Child's correct pronunciation and writing.
2 Mum said I had to use **soap** on my face.
We ate a **loaf** of bread for lunch.
My Gran always **moans** if it is cold.
The children love to row the **boat**.

3
oad words	oast words	oat words
load	coast	boat
toad	roast	coat
road	toast	goat

4 Child's own sentence using an **oa** word.

oo words
Page 20
1 Child's correct pronunciation and writing.
2 The pony had a sore **hoof**.
The **moon** shone through my window at night.
The party **food** looked tasty.
My dog dug up the flower's **roots**!

3
oon words	oom words	oot words
moon	room	boot
soon	broom	shoot
spoon	zoom	root

4 Three of the child's own **oo** words.

ar and er words
Page 21
1 Child's correct pronunciation and writing.
2 summer jar bark card dinner letter
3 The (carpenter) lost his (hammer.) It was found in the (car) (parked) in the (farmyard.)
4 Child's own **ar** and **er** words.

or and ur words
Page 22
1 Child's correct pronunciation and writing.
2 burn curl torn fork fort hurt
3 A (torch) was needed to see the (hurt) (horse) lying next to the (church) on the (turf.)
4 Child's own **or** and **ur** words.

ow words
Page 23
1 Child's correct pronunciation and writing.
2 down – town
how – cow
owl – prowl
3 The **clown** is funny.
The **owl** flew towards the moon.
Pearson has a **brown** coat.
4 Two of the child's own **ow** words.

oi words
Page 24
1 Child's correct pronunciation and writing.
2 boil – soil
join – coin
joint – point
voice – choice
3 Hannah's garden was (spoilt) when the (soil) was flooded. She had no (choice.) She had to wait until it had dried.
4 Two of the child's own **oi** words.

ear words
Page 25
1 Child's correct pronunciation and writing.
2 Picture correctly labelled with ear, beard and tear.
3 Ali's school was **near** to his house.
Anna could **hear** her mum calling.
Terry felt **fear** as he woke in the dark room.
4 Two of the child's own **ear** words.

air words
Page 26
1 Child's correct pronunciation and writing.
2 pair, chair and stair linked to their correct pictures.
3 A brush with (fair) (hair) has fallen down the (stairs) and landed on a (chair.)
4 Child's own sentences using the two listed **air** words.

nk, nd and ng words
Page 27
1 Child's correct pronunciation and writing.
2 sink sand ring ink king hand
3 Table completed with **nk**, **nd** and **ng** words.

l blends
Page 28
1 Child's correct pronunciation and writing.
2
bl words	fl words
blot	flat
blob	flip
pl words	**sl words**
plum	slam
plus	slug

3 Jason found a **slug** in the garden.
Amber ate a **plum** as a snack.
4 Child's own words beginning with the **l** blends.

r blends
Page 29
1 Child's correct pronunciation and writing.
2
dr words	gr words
drop	gran
drag	grip
pr words	**tr words**
pram	trip
prod	trot

3 Kate pushed the baby in the **pram**.
Mr Mead's class went on a **trip** to London.
4 Child's own words beginning with the **r** blends.

s blends
Page 30
1 Child's correct pronunciation and writing.
2
sn words	sp words
snail	spin
snap	spot
st words	**sw words**
stop	swim
step	swing

3 Chloe played on the **swing** (or **step**).
" **Stop!**" shouted the policeman.
4 Child's own words beginning with the **s** blends.

Words to learn
Page 31
1 **Have** **we** eaten **all** the sweets?
Joe looked **for** a ball.
You said he could **have** a drink.
Shall **we** wait **for** them?
They all went **for** a walk.
2 Child's own sentences using the words provided.